SALVADOR DALI

LEAPS OUT OF FRAME

PROSE POETRY BY
PRIYAN

ISBN
Paperback: 979-8-89446-098-7
Hardcase: 979-8-89498-884-9

About the Author

PRIYAN born in Kolkata.

Educated in Kerala & Kolkata

Career Exposure in Aviation, Tourism, Career -Training and Advertising segments

- Widely Travelled in India and Abroad
  - Published two Title in Tourism related subjects
  - Tourism Discovered and Tourism Directory of India
- Published Short Story Collection in Malayalam – Title 'HINDUTHWA'
- Maiden poetry collection

Title - Salvador Dali leaps out of frame

Married to Rose Mary (Well known Writer)

Children – Aravind, Sidharth, Aparna

All settled Abroad

Lives at, 115-P.T.P. Nagar, Trivandrum-695038

Email: priyanoomman@gmail.com   M: 8129097575

Dedicated to my

Dear

Father & Mother

Whispering Words

Light has swallowed darkness

With candles as meek spectators

And our tongues are boneless,

Shameless, But not tasteless

These are verses penned over a span of a decade, at turbulent junctures, introspective interludes, and amid pensive moments of life.

Buddha would have termed

Red as the color of intense desire

Alas, abject desire is evil

and hurdle to nirvana

One could draw each one's life to a vast canvas. Each one trying to draw, distinct images. One wishes to complete the drawing, before our feeble exit. Each one of us draw images which are the reflections of our chequered life. An epitaph of our existential dilemma.

When the travesty of life turn as bewildered and blemished, we juggle with words as escapades and embrace silence for solace.

Love sweats in summer

and swings in spring

Love sprouts with sunrise

and withers with sunset

Stringed temptations are dangled as escape chutes. Black holes are escapades for planets. They may not reaper in cosmos. But we may appear and disappear as penance for purification.

We live and linger in grand numbers. Numbers acquire the numbness to succumb. Reflections tame us to live with anguish. Long live the glory of mirrored myths.

In my verses, literary devices turned handy; string of ironies, similes, metaphors, alliterations and more.

I present my verses for word lovers to evaluate, introspect and relish.

Contents

About the Author   3

Whispering Words   7

Salvador Dali
Leaps Out of Frame   13

Body Language   15

Ardha Nareeshwar   18

Tantric Nirvana   20

Angel Fish   22

Salt Essence   24

Designer Life   26

Measured Moods   28

New Year Notations   30

The Love Grammar   33

Designated Prey   35

Wings of Wine   37

Sailing with Snails   39

Pain Parameters   41

Brand Breath   43

Number Game   45

Malabar's Hidden Treasures	47
Hegemony Patterns	49
Spice of Life	51
Beware of Constipation	53
Spreading Radiance	55
The Eternal Savior	57
Mirror Myths	59
The Unknown Journey	62
Bubbling Bell	66
Angilina's Robotic Love	69
Web worth	71
An Interlude with Madness	72
Gigolo Portrait	74
Illogical Logic	76
Rainbow Inheritance	78
Self Portrait	80
Detachment Destiny	82
Candid Candles	84
Cocktail	85
Poetic Perceptions	*87*

Salvador Dali
Leaps Out of Frame

I have kept a clock and portrait of Dali

On the central wall of my meditation room

Dali mischievously looks at me

And bends the clock needles

The needles lurch in pain and scream

Hey, the time will come to a stand still

Dali retorts yes I wanted to test its patience

Dali places the moon in the lap of sun

The stars fade away with a frown

Days and night cease to appear

Sun and moon play hide and seek

Dali wears a mischievous smile

I search for the lost days and night

I evaporate under his satanic gaze

Dali floats over the melting mist

God stops him in between earth and heaven

'Now, stop your idiotic pranks

I am the one and only supreme creator'

My designs and patterns are irrevocable

Do you want castigated for the trespassing

Dali looked heavenwards and responded

'God, you gave me the power to surpass

Isn't innovation the soul of creativity

Why can't I redraw patterns and parameters

Or if you feel uncomfortable, command my exit'

Suddenly I heard the sound of thunderstorm

The day was restored and the clock with its pace

Dali was pulled back into the portrait frame

He had a large lit sarcasm on his face

And I got thrown out of my meditation

Body Language

My body knew my language

That was ages back

First toned with the language of innocence

That was the most blissful period

I could express emotions raw

The power to weep, love, hate

The power to exhibit hunger day dream and sleep

I could befriend the forbidden world

With innocence my eyes looked irresistible

The warmth of innocence glowed

Like a halo over my head.

With innocence I would be adventurous

The hurdles always buckled under my stare

In the second stage, I lost my innocence

I was being moulded and conditioned

I had my lips with half smile and half frown

The eyes, nose, face, pair of hands, forehead skin

All perplexed over the apt role to play

My soul was unhappy and mind wavering

In my third stage I looked unknown

I lived with a stranger within me

Now I could totally betray my feelings

Now I could hate smiling smooth

1 could enact love with bitterness

Act loyal with traitor traits

My transformations as a versatile actor

With the fire fury hidden in a melting goblet

Walking down the path of a fugitive

Leaving behind no faint footprints

I felt the agony of ignominy

I staged a comeback in my fourth stage

To be on my own, to rediscover my innerself

I was stranger to my mind and soul

I had to reassert the hegemony over my body

I had to bath and to glow in my innocence

I had to breathe the air of sublime purity

My head had to conquer halo

It was an intense struggle to reclaim the glory

Finally I did miraculously succeed

It was a tryst with tranquility for the body, mind, soul

Body can't express any stable longing

Without concurrence of mind and soul

Mind can corrupt the temper of feelings

The soul stare helpless and unsalvageable

The body gets a language what it deserves

The algebra of the body stumbles to retain its core self

But this may not ideally jell with worldly ways

Yes, I should transcend the world of cultivated barriers

Ardha Nareeshwar

Man hidden in a woman

Woman hidden in a man

Massequality, a facade to feminity

Feminity as mask to Massequality

Mother cajoles her son

To weep and weep over sorrows

Don't hold back, reveal fragility

Brood, giggle, burst and cry Like an earthly woman

Reflect the trials and tribulations

Of our motherly nature

The girl looked at her father

With strange deft intensity

How would I ape his masculinity

Could I shave without bristles

Or would I end up shaving off

My shy frivolous charm

How about an impatient hungry look

For picking up frivolous animosity

Man broods on his chivalry

Women sink in her vanity

Man and women share a destiny

Of mutual apprehension and oppression

They drink the spirit of life

And spit fire and douse them

With spilling sweat beads

Strange bed fellows of love and hate

Man and women should be

Reborn with a single body

But with twin mind and soul

The mind and soul will reconcile to

The whims and fancies of the body

Tantric Nirvana

Divine Hot-Line for cherished Nirvanas

Mantras may matter

But are no matches for tantras

Tantric ritual path

Takes on a fast track

To the destiny, nirvana

The unknown manifestation

Of tantra identifies with mysteries

In tantra our left body is negative

And right body with positive invocations

To harness the cosmic energy

One has to overcome the negative vibes

Tantric power has to be evolved within

For which one has to be fearless

And summon strength to face naked power

Tantra is to regiment the forces of nature

Which if untamed could feel terrifying

Tantra is the essence of universal energy

An occult path for infinite realization

Tantra calls for abject self surrender

To the depths of gushing - sweeping energy

Tantra opens- up to an evolving void world

To meditate, sink and dissolve

The aim of life is to demystify

The grammar of our known existence

And the mystery of our unknown exit

Climp spiral stars of nirvana with your shadow

Mask your trails and tribulations

God can't reject our blunt earnestness

Welcome to the exit through tantra

Angel Fish

With our angelic look

We could enthrall the family

In a glass jar

We swam briskly

As we were in the ocean

Our food was insipid

We got bored with the

Fake surroundings

We were sick of life

We were brought up

With vivid expectations

How do we enthrall

How do we enchant

Our growth is stunted

Our world is confused, confined

Our future is to grope in darkness

All because of our angelic looks

There is no escape

The end with dark tunnels

We have been starving for days

Today we expect an end together

Angles have their choices only in heaven

Salt Essence

Salt on your wounds

Burns like charcoal

Salt induces thirst

Quench thirst with blood

Blood tastes sour and salty

Salt sustains life and death

Salt provokes abject anger

Oceans churn out mountains of salt

To sanitize the earth with waves of life

Long live the soul of saintly salt

As, preserver and destroyer

Don`t rub salt on my wounds

Wounds are not self inflicted

Time and space have played their part.

With salt rubbed, pain could be enhanced

Pains have their own rhythmic patterns

Ascending and descending with dexterity.

Salt reposes faith in the sinner

The saints evade the enamor of salt

Guilt tastes salty, and compassion sweet

We are the salt and substance of earth

Salt has an eerie inner strength

Salt has courage and valour

The heart gets jittery with salt

The brain gets jaded with salt

The ocean erupts in salt

The sky tastes the wind of salt

With Salt, taste buds swings in ecstasy

Designer Life

Draw estranged patterns
Which flirt and flip out life
Genome map has zigzag steps
Conjured to weave a designer life

Live in lengthily
Live in broadly
Live in circles
Live in triangles
Live in steps
Live in multiples
Live in heights
Live in depths

Live in awe
Live in illusions
Live in envy
Live in rage
Live in animosity

Live in innocence

Live in melancholy

Live in infinity

Live in absurdity

Live in valley

Live in deserts

Live in water

Live in space

Live up to your dreams

Burn out in lush aspirations

Resurrect with virgin vision

And vaporize in a fiery mission

Measured Moods

All circles are in good shape

Circles exude feminine charm

Circles have multiple layers of sensitivity

Circles don't shrink or succumb

Shape of a square is cosy and homely

Square puts up a show of perfectness

Squares are composed and tidy

Square looks healthy and hearty

Squares are secure with corner guards.

With square, you are sure of past and present

Triangle looks up to the sky for inspiration

Triangle corners you with little charm to escape

Triangle leaves you with less options for progression

Triangle is detached, deliberate and lazy

Triangle has a sharp, envious anatomy

Triangle is mischievous and melancholic

Look at this shape and bewildered patterns

Hexagon is mysterious and magical

Hexagon combines both the male and female aura

Hexagon is a temple couched in faith

Hexagon-looks upward, downward and sideward

Hexagon is the abode of the body mind and soul

Rectangles are shy and meek

Rectangles don't surprise or inspire

Rectangles are unromantic and static

They lie motionless and spiritless

Rectangles metamorphoses into squares

All measures jumble in a circle

Circle encompasses, the square

Rectangle, triangle and hexagon

Moods are condemned to oscillate

Between tightly measured patterns

They stretch to conquer unmeasured patterns

New Year Notations

Cool down Sunil

I know you had an awful year

Which has stolen your glow

You lost your father

Quite an untimely exit

Leaving behind question marks,

Comas, semicolon, dots and void

He lived only for forty eight years

Years of struggle in the dark tunnel

With four children and a shadow wife

With four jobs and two serious ailments

He was in search for money and warmth

Care, belonging, dignity and God

Sunil you lost your mother at a young

Young age, you hardly remember

Your step mother with her own child

Was not kind with care, concern

You grew like an orphan

But with burning ambition

To survive, succeed and proclaim

It looked like your were on the

Accomplishing streak track

But with the accident you got crippled

The new year could bestow on you

12 months of hope

52 weeks of fruity anticipations

365 days of nudging bliss

8760 hours of edgy cheer

52000 minutes of near misses

Now cool down Sunil.

Lets us welcome the new year

Time can't bend to stay static

It has to move forward

It can't look backward

Why keep brooding over the past

Why don't we live in future

Future gives us a sense of anticipation

Future gives us hope and solace

Sunil, awake, summon courage, cheer-up

The sun is rising in East and West

Looks like it is changing the pattern

Let us redraw our patterns of sorrows

The Love Grammar

Love floats in the air

Love makes waves in the ocean

Love roars across the infinite space

Love has a date with the rainbow

Rainbow fades with promise to reappear

The colours flirt and flair, mate and melt

Make your loved ones dance to your tune

Like a peacock with blooming feathers

True love ensures surrender

How does one express love

Love smells sweet and sour

Love tastes salty and fiery

It needs nourishment, water, light, and breeze

Sunlight brightens moonlight soothes

Find out what's in store for love life

Dream in the past, toil in the present,

Succumb and burnout in the future

How does one survive the loss of love

Being in search for eternal love

The art of selfless love

Let the heart weep, wander, prey

For those who lost the love game

Words can fail to express your love

Expressions can fail to transmit your love

Deeds can fail to transcend your love

Love sprouts with sunrise and withers in sunset

Love swings in spring and sweats in summer

Designated Prey

The spider spins the web in an intricate pattern

The prey could take a nap till the spider bestows redemption

But spider is unsure of how long the web would stay

Any human species could erase it with playful indulgence

The spider's prayers are answered with dutiful preys

We are like cunning spiders waiting for

The assigned prey to perch on the web

We don't swallow, we nibble, pierce, scratch or smell them.

The victim prey returns only to disappear

Once on the web you get intoxicated with illusions

We have the pleasure of slowly being eaten up

We disappear unconscious without pangs of death

Here the spider lives till eternity

The information junkyard is the fodder for us

All information gets stale and stagnant.

We keep discovering more and more information

We feel reinvented with new information

We are terrified with the size and range of information.

But with little choice we wish to be part of a knowledge society

Knowledge gives us appetite to conquer space and mind

The conquering spirit elopes with the charged body

The soul has to wait till death, for true liberation.

Wings of Wine

Solomon sang song of songs

With heady wine of Lebanon

The wine yards of Lebanon

Gets nurtured by the celestials

Queen Shebha swam like a nymph

In blue waters of Mediterranean sea

Mesmerized with Solomon's gaze

Inhale the air of resurrection

Wine purifies the toxic blood

It washes away our guilt

Wine helps the body to bloom

It prods the mind to swing

Wine wings on doubtful lovers

They float on the hidden clouds

Only to reappear with zest for ecstasy

Wine wakes you up to twilight

With, blushing moon trying to sneak in

Wine ferments in your melancholy

Drink it when faith leaps skyward

Wine could unshackle your bonds

It sets your soul free for ultimate sojourn

Sailing with Snails

Snails are mostly in prayfull mood

Pleading accommodation and tolerance

Like the tortoise they too have

A shell to hide their pride

Only to appear in alien darkness

And disappear in merciless day light

Their pace is peaceful and thoughtful

They are in awe of human species

Resigned in pleading with shrunken gestures

We are charmed by butterflies, fireflies

But they too are celestial creations

Snails are left with fervent prayers

May evolution evolve us into bewitching

Fairy looks and fiery fantasy

Faith condones rebirth with a choice

A choice with lingering aspirations

Aspiring to be loved, not despised

Redemption propels your esteem

Sinners qualify for redemption

Snails have an ardent date with salvation

Pain Parameters

Pain redefines patience and tolerance

Pain could even purify the temptations

Pain is a mirage and imposing truth

Pain could lead the way to martyrdom

A body and mind which can't feel pain

Floats in zero gravity with numbness

The essence of life is unveiled through pain

Pains have their own rhythmic patterns

Conquer fear for trespassing pain

Mask the intense pain with steely will

But it will return in all its ferocity

Then one reels and wriggles under acute pain

Pain wave lengths, crawl upon you

Like a burning thundering fireball

Pains are born with inauspicious signs

They exit only on the altar of death

Pain have taught us to forgive and forget

Pain have taught us to fathom pleasure

Pain like death is a great leveler

Pain parades before us like a savior

Pain paves the way to resurrection

Pain triggers your faith on death

Which would make you flutter and float

In the air like floating feather

Brand Breath

Client: Breathe life into my brand

Pump fresh blood into its veins

Chisel it into an alluring shape

Inject hormones to refresh its aura

Instill trust into its essence

Deck it up with psychedelic colours

Cream it up with morning dew

Prop it up on top of the cliff

Agency: The brand is dormant and dicey

The brand is dormant and toothless.

It has to be re-launched with value additions

The corporate brand image has also faded

First the corporate image is to be reinforced

Let the consumer re-evaluate and summon trust

Instilling trust is a herculean task

The product has to earn trust

Trust has the power to move mountains

The target: We are living in an age at flickering trust and loyalty

Our parents and grandparents were loyal

But then, they lived in a choice less world

Endless choices hoodwinks choice less relationships

Summary: The redundant brand has seven rivals

All of them better and brighter

Give us an unbeatable vivid lure

Trigger before the time runs out

We are all galloping into the timeless zone

Number Game

One has the quality of oneness

Two turns the scene into twilight

Three gets into the threshold of thrifty

Four fumes with fiery frenzy

Five fathoms the depths of moods

Six acquaints the fortune on despair

Seven saviors the seven samurais

Eight engulfs the ageing heritage

Nine networks with worldly web

Ten takes off into luminous horizon

Twenty has a vigorous vigour

Twenty five has a silver halo

Thirty has a delicate balance

Forty has a feverish puzzle

Fifty has a mood to meditate

Sixty has a shaken shadow

Seventy serves the survivor

Eighty lapses out in anonymity

Ninety fades and fades in oblivion

Hundred leaps to swallow the zeros

We linger and live in grand numbers

Numbers acquire the numbness to succumb

Malabar's Hidden Treasures

Malabar weaves fiery strands

Triggered into one giant tale

A mix of numerous fables

Striding over centuries of heritage

Delivering one exquisite experience

When does a story loose its punch

That happens when a rival story

Descends with a deadly punch

The fossils of the phoenicians.

The testaments of the chosen jews

Arabs with their desert zest

Greeks descending from appollo

Romans galloping on chariots

Vasco da Gama prowling for Portuguese

The Dutch encoded with the Vikings DNA

French imbibing the spirit of Napoleon

And at last the English for their bread and butter

Malabar for them in myriad hues and colors

The algebra of spices, the essence of vibes

The arithmetic of conquest, the art of deception

The voidness of the valour, the vividness of virtue

In between St Thomas float ashore with a chosen cross.

Islam followed with unshakeable faith

Malabar with a heady cocktail of fantasy fables and spices

Malabar with the kallai timber, kalari and ethnic damsels

The uru floating in Arabian sea with pepper and cinnamon.

With the oars tuned by the masked virgins

Over Malabar the sky is overcast with amorous clouds

Hegemony Patterns

Stand up, now sit down

Turn around and run around

Why do I feel uncomfortable

Because I have no option

Either I obey or I quit

The words are emphatic and cold

The choice is couched between wails

One turns around and runs

Around for close identity

Creating patterns of common fraternity

I feel at times that someone

Should command over me

When I don't make any choices

Don't listen to what others say

Listen to your inner voice

The inner voice murmurings with feeble voice

We have logic and reason

To blackout our inner glow

Does one bestow the power of glory to our soul

For establishing hegemony over our self

Hegemony harbors hate and awe

It flutters its feathers on the gullible horizon

Hegemony emit fury, fire and fear

Hegemony surrenders to the power of love and empathy

Spice of Life

Spiraled ladder of life

Like the intricate genome

With hip hop hazards

Jells with jealous ginger

Ginger jives gently

With jelly filled envy

The acid tongue gulps

The timely curse with pretence

Salty moods sullen

With blooming platitudes

Words turn frozen

With fragile taste buds

Sour coats the voice with

Cinnamon scented saliva

Chilly chirps in majestically

To provocative docile thoughts

The breath burns in revolt

Sweetness douses the fire

With tact and telepathic smile

Sweetness resolves to capture the spirit

How would life be spiceless and spineless

Climb up the spiraled ladder

To discover the strange patterns

Astronomical progression to the unknown

Will future term this as the spice of life

Beware of Constipation

Half the wars fought on earth

Were on account of perennial constipation

Constipation triggers envy and animosity

It extinguishes lingering tranquility

Constipation ruins the appetite for life

It shreds our calm and compassion

Devil conspires with constipation

To torpedo the divine connectivity

Buddha, Christ and Krishna ate little

Had consciously averted constipation

As they had larger missions to fulfill

Hitler, Mussolini, Polpot, and more

Annihilated millions on constipated rage

Constipation radiates ire and irritation

Its swallows the source of reason

Karl Marx with hunger and constipation

Could deliver das capital only with super will

That was a conspiracy to redraw history

Food will contaminate thoughts

Thoughts lead to starvation

Starvation helps to elude constipation

Long live the life of lofty thoughts sans constipation

Spreading Radiance

The lady looked around

Her neck holding her oval face

Went round round and round

Her lengthy hair like a merry goes around

Concealing the unshapely skull

The shapely legs were holding her body

With poise and elegant patterns

The feet looked fairy and fabulous

She was woven in sprinkled petals

And washed in the milky rivulets

Spreading radiance is no joke

How does one define radiance

The depth and sparkle of eyes

The posture of sharpened nose

The featherlike soft ears

The cascading hair and forehead

The firm lips shielding lust

The arch eyebrows with vulnerable sheen

The hands eerie hastily and stately

The palm fleshy and flamboyant

Come have a close look at her face

Did you feel the emitting radiance

Did you hear the sound of sanguinity

The lady was in introspection

The protective soul reassured, don't worry

I am your soul, indestructible and impeccable

The lady will radiate the spark of her soul

All souls are left with inner radiance

The Eternal Savior

All are in the look out for a Savior

A Savior who anointed to sacrifice

A Savior who could wash our sins

Sins accumulate on the altar of life

Sins with signs of decay

Eating the enclaves of our soul.

The Savior steps out of heaven

Looks down with a heavy heart

How do I save them

Should I trigger an earthquake

Hurricane, molten lava, floods or fire

Each soul is craving for an escape

Earth has turned to be a monumental cross

We play cross words to coin password

Password opens up a world of probable

One should transcend the agony of temptations

Temptations open up new vistas of discovery

Discovery leads to disillusion

Disillusion harbors negation

Negation perpetuates sin and guilt

Mirror Myths

How do we live

Without a mirror

Reflecting our bloated image

Images are evolved

How does one build an image

How could one shatter an image

Mirror reflects the shadow

Shadow with dark halo

Mirror mesmerises the self

Mirror echoes the ego

Mirror sanitises the reality

Mirror fathoms truth

Mirror images complexities

And camouflage entity

Each day we wake up to recheck

In the mirror for flickering life

Mirror admonishes the aged

And plays with childish innocence

Women bloom in the mirror

And abandon their fragility

They bloat and float in the air

With perplexed aura in the mirror

Look into the mirror with vengeance

Vengeance to overcome the wounds

In my tender trembling age

In the faded broken mirror

I could see fragmented feelings

Broken love, anger, envy and ecstasy

In life we spend hours in front of a mirror

Only to reassure our shell and emptiness

Mirror manipulates the reflection

Caricatured images are self tortures

Mirror drowns us with a painful mask

We unmask when not mirrored

It is scary to look into the mirror in midnight

You could look like an impoverished ghost

Mirror yearns to propel the inner soul

The reflections do not justify, testify

Your orphaned self exiled testimony

Long live the terror of reflections

Long live the glory of mirrored myths

The Unknown Journey

We embark on an eventful journey
From the unknown to the unknown
It covers many mile stones
Marked with guilt, curse and introspection

I fall into the trap of child hood memory
The train crosses river Godavari
Torrential rain trashes the bogies
There are country boats with flickering lanterns
While the moon disappears behind the clouds
Rajahmundry station the bastion of Tenali Raman
Platform frozen with guards swaying green light
I stay awake to watch the mango groves
Large shadows of mango trees
A line of ghosts with a fruitful mission

I am placed on the lower berth with dreams

My father walks and looks at distance.

His large face in the company of shifting shadows

The journey for us, as inevitable and eternal

We trespass valleys, mountains, rivers and deserts

We trespass the future, present and past

We trespass the signs, omens and oracles.

I woke up with mature dreams

The train was negotiating the terrain

The terrain harbors hordes of cactus

Cactus spells the nectar of hope

Train was slowly crawling in to green symphony

The spell of life vitality sprung up vividly

The journey keeps us hopeful

The journey from birth hood to death hood

In between we weep, laugh, sulk, brood, brawl and bite

We have edgeless envy, compassion, guilt and love

The journey evolves, and dissolves into evolution

It penetrate into the path of discoveries

Journey starts from alien cliff

The journey ends up in a valley with wild flowers

The train grazes through the paddy fields

The stokes fly in unison into the horizon

The wetlands glitter in the dawn sunlight

We disembark into cold reality

The car drives us into the past

My grandfather holds my hand tightly

He looks fragile with piercing eyes

He connects the past with future

Grandfather exudes smell of antiquity

With the temper of depth and warmth

He guides us to bible's new testament

With the invocation of old testaments

The transformation from rage to compassion

My father left us with grandpa

And shortly left the world reassured

Poor soul, I felt sorry for my grandpa

Wailing and wailing like an old testament prophet

True, the journey begins with pregnant expectation

All journeys are expected to deliver eventful encounters

We embark on a journey of emancipation

We are born to live and die in hope

Hope to trigger us with hope to live

Perhaps a journey from the unknown

Bubbling Bell

Jingle bells, jingle bells

Jingle all the way

How I wonder the wish to sway

The school bell rings

To end and start learning

Start and end with mixed

Expectation and feelings

The church bell tolls

Echoing the sound of death

The bells chime in unison

To usher the divine energy

The auctioneer shakes the bell

To fix the benefactors

Bells ring and awake us from slumber

They initiate us to the auspicious temper

Bells have a cute sound shape

They have an inbuilt aura of their own

With bells you can expect the unexpected

They store abundant measure of sound

They enact, the final retreat with self torture

The blue - bells blossom for the day

They only look like bells with sound of silence

We have string of cute bells, swayed by the breeze

It doesn't awake the birds, lizards or even the cats

Bells have been created to please the gods.

The Notre Dame Cathedral tower has a

Giant church bell glowing and glittering

The tongue of the bell weighing high

It could even wake up entire Paris

Echoing the spirit of Victor Hugo

And his hero Quasimodo of Notredame with hunch

The bell also heralded the coronation of Napoleon

The architect of Europe's apolitical edifice

The bell also unveiled the sounds of French revolution

With the dream of equality, fraternity and freedom

Jingle bells, jingle bells

Jingle all the way

How I wonder the wish to sway

Angilina's Robotic Love

Pygmalion, the Greek sculptor god fell in love
With his own exquisite creation Galatea
Goddess Venus had to breath life into Galatea
To avert the self destruction threat of Pygmalion

David living in AD 2030 married robot Angilina
David the futuristic bio- engineer designer
Took more than five years to create Angilina
He took enormous pain and had immense patience
In this path breaking passionate creation

Robot Angilina had curious traits of his
Mother, sister Rebeca, and wife Jovan
Body, face, eyes, skin, hair, ears, lips, all identical
Angilina was aptly evolved to be
Charming, radiant, affectionate and loving

David had already Jovan as his wife

Jovan and David were in and out of love for some time

They found the going tough with stale and pale turns

Jovan found a way out, why not a second marriage

David could marry a robot of his own creation

The robot would not be a threat ever

What a marvelous turn to have a predestined life

David, Jovan and Angilina lived together ever after

Of course Angilina would outlive them as an orphan

If David wouldn't don the role of a destroyer

Web worth

What is your networth when you are hooked to net

Webwealthy, webwise, websavvy, webweary

The giant web many times larger than the planet

Covering the intricate mass of the world

Weighing the networth of each one of us.

We have little choice; we are trapped

We are wrapped, rigged braid and bound

The all pervading power of web

Would turn us into freaks and neurotics

Web transforms things into virtual reality

We would live in virtual space

Virtual love, hatred, animosity, compassion

The only exceptions would be death and birth

We will have no privacy from foe or friend

A world where nothing to seek or hide

A world with deadly silence and fossilised bodies

We would be wed to digital dilemmas

Enter the age of web worth fantasy

Where each one would be insane robots

An Interlude with Madness

Madness opens the door to spirituality

Madness unfolds the window to creativity

Madness gives us a surreal facade

Nirmalan my friend went mad this spring

What made him mad is anyone's guess

With madness he was looking fresh and innocent

Nirmalan led an abnormal life till thirty three

He forgot his wedding and mothers' death

Now he speaks sense with sparkle in his eyes

Earlier he used to focus on heady stuff like

Philosphy mathematics, and logic

But now eager on bees, cow dung and eyebrows

Now tell me what is madness

Madness hovers, since time immemorial

Even before and after Buddha and Christ

One cannot attain madness at the conscious level

This appears at the subconscious sphere

Madness like death is a great leveler

There is no precaution against madness

Neither could one hinder madness

Moments of madness breathes life into poetry

Madness screams like a thunderbolt

Madness weeps like a morning due

Madness rides on the waves of voidness

It bridles the sense of logic and reason

Madness reflects on the mirror, perplexed

And the reflection on the water turns hostile

Nirmalan is forced to come out of his madness

But he fears to remain sane

In madness he could float like a bird

Swim like a fish, roam like a squirrel

Roar like a lion and erupt like a volcano

Pose like a rainbow weep like the monsoon

Now Nirmalan is being cleansed

He is adamant on remaining mad

You can't mix sanity with insanity

Sane specious should stay together

For them, it is dangerous to stretch boundaries

Dangerous to wander purposeless and perplexed

Gigolo Portrait

I am Anand with 27 years of life

A college dropout with a dancing body

I have provoking muscles all over the body

I have piercing looks and a sweet tongue

Pubs, discos, style spots, malls, plush hotels are my domain

Anand could be a dancer, actor, model, stripper or sucker

He wears bewitching perfumes, which women can't resist

He has an i-phone, fossil watch, calvinklein innerwear

He wears pierre cardin, gucchi, police and platinum cross

Today he has a date with Sunitha

Weighing 46 years with two children and an elusive husband

She frowns and fumes in her designer apartment

Anand services her ardently, eminently

Sunitha weeps with her naked body

Anand hugs, cuddles tickles and swings

She holds on like a leech, breathing lust of life

Anand exposed, and exasperated, resurrect her body

Sunitha transcends ecstasy and recapture ego

Anand, you are rewarded with money, diamonds, pride

You have quenched my lust and salvaged my soul

This will empower my spirit to stay on and on

Anand's mobile sang, it was an impatient Renuka

She could be cruel and demanding and of course paying

Anand for a while thought of his estranged mother

How could a mother deny her son for two decades

Renuka resembled his mother except the harshness

She had no tenderness left for committed gigolos

They could take pride in their body but not over their soul.

Illogical Logic

Why is life beyond our logic

Is it because it is God's logic

Does our logic and reasoning

Melt like ice in front of God's will

His is infinite and beyond logic

Life in myriad forms and their destiny

Rights and wrongs are imposed on us

God has no role in our do's and don'ts

You are known as a survivor, savior or sinner

Look beyond logic of sin and guilt

Heaven and hell, fear and greed

Where one could experience the dogma of divine

Life flirts with logic and illogic

To measure the depths of heaven and hell

They are twilight paths for us to pursue

We live and die in hope

For us hopes are sane and sacred

Hope revolves around perplexed logic

Induce us with a slice of fresh rainbow

We have more to track, before we reap

Rainbow Inheritance

Women encompass the fragrance, colour, moods of nature

They inherit its sweat, blood empathy and compassion

She looked for the rains to lash against her mood swings

She had to meet her paramour in the train

The train would take them up to the mountains

She always loved to hide in the mountain lap

He had lost his mother as a child.

He grew up in hostels as father was indifferent

He had a hidden energy source

Drawing energy from her probing life

She had lots and lots of unreserved energy

She feels women are the true inheritors of earth

Earth manifests the essence of femininity

She can now feel the hidden strength

She was possessed with mystical powers

They are now on the cliff of the mountain

They can touch and feel the clouds

They can straighten the rainbows

Now on, the rainbows would not vanish

Self Portrait

With such flat nose

One could frown endless

With large luminous eyes

One could invoke expectations

With large forehead

One could convey depth

With mean shapeless ears

One could part uneasiness

With thick ruffian lips one could convey stiffness

With long thick legs

One could look provoked

With long stretching hands with thick fleshy palms

One could look contrived

With flat heavy foot

One could look earthly with a square face

One could have endless expressions

With a heavy torso

One could stride and scare surroundings

With a huge comfortable buttocks

One could look steady and static

We can draw our own portrait

Self portrait could deceive our reflections

Detachment Destiny

Is detachment deliberate

Yes, if it helps you escape the bond

But why does one get into bonds

Because bonding gives a sense of shelter

Detachment, makes you float

Floating like a bird with open options

Attachment holds with prearranged patterns

Detachment adorns uncertain patterns

Detachment could be callous and cruel

Attachment makes us vulnerable and soft

The predicament of life is to cave in

Sacrifices endears life's mission

For the heart to swell, forego all that is guarded

Attachment could perpetuate disillusion

Feelings flourish in evolving attachment

All fundamentals in nature are attached

But they could also turn detached out of choice

One turns detached with trials and tribulations

With detachment you could probe the alien path

Detachment gives you a sublime vision

Traversing beyond the self sustained goals

Detachment determines the pursuit to probe

The choice of destiny could be chosen

The choice is to dwell deeper into the unknown

Detachment bestows freedom on martyrdom

Candid Candles

Candle burns

Eating up darkness

Light spreads with vehemence

Shadows lurk in fear

Life fades with shaky shape

Candles burns out

Darkness spreads the blanket

Life disappears like an obedient child

Cocktail

Scrape your mood

Chop your words

Mince your thoughts

Stir your dreams

Scramble your sighs

Shake your words with lime

Coat your words with honey

Dry your words with chilly

Chisel your words with thunder

Stretch your words with typhoon

Smell your words with clove

Taste your words with ginger

Munch your words with cardamom

Garnish your spirit with

A heady mouthful cocktail

Poetic Perceptions

Poets becomes the litmus test of a society with it composite diversities. The aesthetics of poetry is always a point of contention. Poetic sensibilities could be influenced by factors like Geography, race, life, cultural nuances, faith, language, gender equations, identity, ecology, suffering, philosophy, psychology, spirituality and much more.

In poetry there is room for experimentation with form style and content. Poetic language carries the imprint of the poet's intrinsic identity.

Poetry mostly aims to relive our collective memory. Nostalgia has the power to tame our tempered feelings. Memoirs come out vivid and vibrant in poetry. Evocative poetry, with the flavor of wistful sentiments and deep introspection jolts the reader to emotional depths.

Creativity is fountainhead of life. Fantasy evolves into ideation, ideation to ideology or doctrine. They trigger fresh inventions, discoveries and revelations. Today, ideators are opinion makers and path breakers.

Poetry trigger tremors and tribulations the symmetry of language and raises divergent dimensions to existing meanings. New words and expressions evolve to address the emerging perceptions of communication.

With the changing times, poetry has also taken liberty in embracing thematic changes and transforming the dynamics of language.

Great poetry transcends time and space. They are ethereal and eternal. Yes poetry being timeless, will always remain relevant and rejuvenating.

The poems encased here, interfaces on a range of experiences and themes. We approach life with a certain plan and pattern. It could go haywire with evolving complicities and conflicts. In our journey, in most junctures, we compromise. But at certain crucial points, we deviate from the proven path, to discover new vistas and strange insights.